THE SEVEN MINUTE STAR
become a great speaker in 15 simple steps

www.thesevenminutestar.com

Cover artwork, illustration & composing by www.navarra-design.com

Printed in the United States of America

ISBN 978-1-45059-975-7

ACKNOWLEDGMENTS

Writing the first book is an incredibly enriching experience and a great opportunity for self reflection. I would like to send out some special thank-yous to the following people who helped me bring ***The Seven Minute Star*** to life:

- Special Thanks to Arthur Waters and Claude Desroches for their outstanding work on the editing side.

- Special Thanks to Bart Navarra and his team for giving the book its unique design.

- Special Thanks to Christoph Reisner and Sven-David Müller for helping me on the publishing side.

- Special Thanks to Trent zum Mallen for his everlasting encouragement.

- Special Thanks to Andi Kaim, Román Rosete ten Pas, Ryan Slack, and JK Wasson for their constructive criticism.

- Special Thanks to all my fellow Toastmasters from Prestigious Speakers Barcelona – you guys are phenomenal!

- Special Thanks to Team Europe Ventures, Tony Anagor, and ESEI for their great collaboration in the educational arena.

- Special Thanks to Harry Beckwith for inspiring me with his marketing classic Selling the Invisible (1997).

- Special Thanks to Luis Walter for always believing in me.

- Special Thanks to my family and my Dad†: *"You are the star of my life!"*

— for Rose —

THE SEVEN MINUTE STAR CONTENT

THE CATS MEOW

New Orleans — jazz, Mardi Gras — the historic French Quarter, and the vibrant nightlife! I dived into it when I stopped over on a road trip in 1995. Cats Meow, on Bourbon Street, is a famous karaoke bar. I stood in the crowd admiring the people who dared to step out onto the stage, into the spotlight in front of the raucous crowd. I wanted to sing too, so very much! But — I just couldn't. I was terrified by all those critical eyes out there, staring, judging, sometimes admiring but sometimes booing. I suffered from what we all suffer from: I suffered from stage-fright!

Now it's fifteen years later, and I speak at weddings, at parties, at business meetings. I write songs and perform them. I have created my own public speaking seminar that's both educational and entertaining. And my role as *primus inter pares* of The Festival, a European movement of which I am the initiator and co-founder, often requires that I give informative and inspiring speeches to a wide variety of people, and to different audiences all the time. And I love it! I constantly look for new opportunities to be a *star* – ***The Seven Minute Star***.

You're not looking to be a star? Not for a lifetime? Not for a few years? Not even for just a few months, or weeks, or days? Not even for — seven minutes?

Fine. No problem. I didn't write this to turn you into a star — but I do mean for this book to inspire you, so sometimes you can feel like a star.

So — A Seven Minute Star? What the heck is that, anyway? Well, what is a star? A star is someone with charisma, with a positive attitude, an engaging spirit, enthusiasm, passion. People admire stars. We celebrate them.

And seven minutes? Seven minutes is the best amount of time for a public speech. There are one hour speeches, 30 minute speeches, and TED[1] talks of 20 minutes, but normally it takes about seven minutes until the first few people in the audience, usually the ones in the last three rows, start to fall asleep. Seven is king!

Stars and public speakers have a lot in common — so whenever you

---

[1] http://www.ted.com

get up to make a speech, to any audience of any size, you will be *The Seven Minute Star*. And if you follow the steps I offer you in this little book, you too will be able to speak, even for 45 minutes, without anyone falling asleep.

THANK YOU, RALPH!

So How Did It Happen?

The answer goes back to the year 1924, when Ralph C. Smedley founded Toastmasters in Santa Ana, California. Today it is Toastmasters International, with local clubs nearly everywhere, all around the world. Toastmasters has changed my life; it has transformed me into an outgoing, extroverted and passionate public speaker — I enjoy what I speak about, and I also simply enjoy the act of speaking in public.

My introduction to Toastmasters came in 2005, when a friend invited me to a meeting of Prestigious Speakers, a local chapter in Barcelona. I signed up right away. *"Wow,"* I thought, *"these people are moving from just plain smart to being so brilliant, they're almost like Aristotle!"*

Toastmasters emphasizes learning by doing, and you do it with people you like. You'll learn

- how to speak;
- how to move your body;
- how to vary your voice, so the people in the last row won't fall asleep;
- how to use supporting visual aids — what we call props;
- how to include catchy anecdotes, quotations, and humor;
- how to maintain eye contact with the entire audience;
- how to structure a speech;
- how to keep your allotted time by speaking less while still making your point; and
- how to engage your audiences enthusiastically.

You'll turn into a passionate speaker, and you'll always have your greatest asset on display: your smile!

This book, *The Seven Minute Star*, is a collection of my own personal experience gleaned not only from spending four years with Toastmasters, but also from applying its lessons in the real world. This book is experience-driven, and offers practical tips and tricks on how to master those seven minutes on stage.

There's a star in each and every one of us — we just have to prepare ourselves, and let that star step out into the spotlight.

I will definitely return to New Orleans, and when I do, I'll head straight for the Cats Meow. I'll climb right up onto the stage, take a deep breath, calm myself, and look deeply into everyone's eyes. Then — with passion — I will sing: *"Start spreading the news…"*

So, Thank you, Ralph! You helped me change my life.

FIFTEEN SIMPLE STEPS

So here we are – YOU are about to become *The Seven Minute Star* — and in just 15 simple steps!

All 15 steps are autonomous learning blocks. If your goal is only to become starlet rather than a fully-fledged seven minute star, you could apply any one of these steps individually, and your speaking style will improve correspondingly.

But of course the secret lies in climbing up all 15 steps, up to the stage, elevating your speaking abilities, growing and expanding, so you'll shine in the spotlight.

The first two steps — *confidence, transparency* — are the foundation of your performance. You need these basic principles to climb up further.

With the third step — *your first sentence* — you'll create that indispensable link of tension between yourself and your audience.

Steps four through seven — *eye contact, voice, body language, visual aids* — keep that tension high and guarantee that no one in your audience falls asleep.

Steps eight to eleven — *structure, rhetoric, anecdotes, quotations* — gives your audience the impression that what they have heard was more than informative, but has actually been profound.

To make your speech truly memorable, though, you need to continue with steps twelve to fourteen — *humor, enthusiasm, passion.* And the final step, both the simplest and the most difficult, the most obvious and the most important, is your *smile.*

Making it unforgettable	Humor	Enthusiasm	Passion	☺
Delivering great content	Structure	Rhetoric	Anecdotes	Quotes
Keeping your audience's attention	Eye contact	Voice	Body language	Visual Aids
Getting everyone to listen	First sentence			
Before you speak	Confidence		Transparency	

Once you've climbed up all 15 steps, you'll be standing on the stage ready for the spotlight. For seven minutes you'll feel like a star. Indeed, you'll be a star, and it will be unforgettable.

So what are you waiting for — let's get started!

STEP ONE
The Cat And The Dogs

Imagine you're a cat. Imagine also — you're giving a speech to an audience of 500 Rottweilers. The term "hostile audience" would have to be redefined! Yet you take on the challenge. You are even thrilled to do it. You step up on stage. The snarling and barking crowd down there might cause you some concern, but rather than being scared, you feel inspired; you're even more enthusiastic, because you know what you have to say is important. You cut through the sound of hostility with a roaring "Meow," and with a firm voice you begin to purr. You are the cat's meow! You can do it because, from your whiskers to the tip of your tail, you are filled with a wonderful essence, the most important quality any public speaker can have: *confidence.*

Search your memory — remember the last time you saw someone speaking in public. Can you picture the scene? Good. Now, how did the speaker look? Nervous? Tense? A little coughing? Did the speech begin with a long and disturbing *"Aahhh — Ummmm"* before an *"OK, well..."* got added, for variety? Was the room still noisy when the speech began? Did the speaker look at the floor, or off to the side, or over everybody's head?

That Darn Stage-Fright!

Stage-fright is one of those things, like fleas, that nobody really needs. Where does it come from? When I was in college, why couldn't I sit in a group of students and just say, *"Hi, I'm Florian, I study Business Administration, and I'm here today to find a great employer,"* without suffering from a dry mouth, sweaty palms and high blood pressure?

Once I attended a seminar about moderating discussions given by my friend Bernhard Pelzer from Hamburg. He explained that, when you're leading a discussion in a larger group, you should always focus on sub-groups of five. This is because a very long time ago we would be sitting in the trees in groups of – you guessed it – five! So, when we were still covered with fur, five was the crucial number. This is now written deep in our brains, in our cerebellum.

But, thanks to Charles Darwin, we did climb down from the trees; we evolved. From that moment on, down from the trees and out in the open, our cerebellum learned to distrust any group of strangers — especially those larger than five; it tells you: *"Those guys over there most likely want to kill you. Shut your mouth and get outta here! NOW!"* So the last thing your cerebellum wants you to do out there in the meadow is to open your mouth and say, *"Hey guys, how are you doing?"*

This hasn't changed. When I was thirteen, I had to perfom a clarinet concert before a large, intimidating, and (to me at least) even menacing audience of 300. I almost wet my pants. I can still hear my cerebellum yelling: *"Run away — NOW!"*

Dear Future Master Speaker: Although this feeling may be real, even hard-wired in, surrendering to it Does Not Work — not for you, not for anyone! Audiences don't want to look at a fearful, anxious creature nearly overcome by nerves. That is exactly what they do not want to see.

You Are The Star
Most of the times we speak in public, there is some sort of stage. You, as a speaker, will stand on that stage, standing up above everyone else, who will be looking up at you. Do you know why stars are called stars? Because we look up at them in the sky. And your audience will be looking up to you. While you are speaking, YOU ARE THE STAR!

Practice, Practice, Practice
I may not be a cat, but sometimes I have felt rather like that cat up in front of an audience of 500 Rottweilers. But now I feel that I can gather up all their leashes into my little paw and pull on them. It establishes a sort of tension between my audience and myself. It puts me in control, and gives me an exhilarating feeling of confidence.

This feeling, confidence, is what has let me say good-bye to stage-fright, so today, I consider every speech an opportunity, not a threat. I love to deliver my personal knowledge to my audiences. I am thrilled to go up there both to educate and to entertain people. Sometimes I even start a speech with a little rapping — and I am definitely not Eminem.

The river of my life has flowed unbroken, from the time I played the clarinet, past my time at the university, all the way through to today. Sometimes it's been torrential, other times calm, sometimes threatening to overflow its banks, sometimes nearly dried up. This river of time is really experience. And if you want to move beyond your fear and gain confidence, then you must jump right in. Practice, practice, practice! Whenever you can, whenever you have the chance, just speak right up and say: *"Here I am! I will speak. Let me speak — NOW!"*

Go ahead and sing in dark, shady karaoke bars — and do the best possible thing for yourself: join a nearby chapter of Toastmasters!

STEP TWO
Diving Into Ice-Cold Water

Jack Lemmon once said: *"If you really do want to be an actor who can satisfy himself and his audience, you need to be vulnerable. You must reach the emotional and intellectual level of ability where you can go out stark naked, emotionally, in front of an audience."*

$15 For Crying

I love this quotation. I believe that at some point great speakers automatically become actors. The speaker, just like the actor, evokes emotions in the audience. When Leonardo DiCaprio froze to death in the ice-cold water of the Atlantic, people all over the world cried waterfalls. They paid up to 15 bucks just so they could have a chance to cry. Positive or negative emotions, happiness and sadness: it's all about connecting with your audience on an emotional level.

Your Weakness Is Their Weakness

Now let me ask you a question: How can you expect to touch your audience's heart if you do not, yourself, open up? An emotional refrigerator will never evoke any reaction in the audience. Yes, they will say, it was an *OK* speech, technically — but that's not even close to the *Wow!* effect.

Many people have a great deal of difficulty with transparency. Too many times I've heard someone say: *"Yes, yes, but I can't open up too much — it could be dangerous for me."*

I say, they're only afraid it would be dangerous. When they say this, they're giving in to their fear — and if you live in fear, you'll never get anywhere.

Look, what kind of people do you think are sitting down there in the audience? Exactly! Human beings, normal people, just like you and me, fearful people, positive people, anonymously alcoholic people, good people, funny people, bad, sad, and mad people, all kinds of people you could ever imagine, and a few that would never even occur to you.

My personal experience has shown me that audiences love you when you share intimate stories about yourself. They can identify with your feelings and weaknesses, and will take heart from your strength — because only strong people can reveal themselves to the world.

The Iceberg Syndrome

Let's forget about speeches for a moment and take a look at another arena in which communication skills are also essential: networking.

Ever since I can remember, my friends have called me 'the socializer'. I have always been deeply interested in getting to know people and their stories. Meeting and talking to strangers is not everyone's passion, but it is mine.

Consider how two strangers normally meet at a cocktail party. I call it the iceberg effect. When A meets B, the only thing each one can see is the tip of the other's iceberg, as it were. Naturally, A says something to B about the weather or a recent movie, and B responds with something about the economy or about the Superbowl. These topics keep them both above the waterline — that is, the conversation stays superficial. (Image 1)

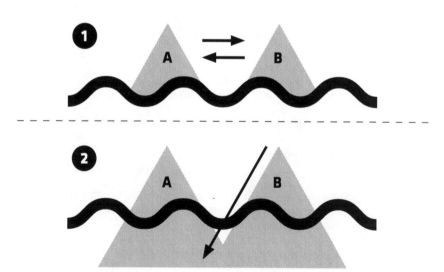

But a passionate networker like B (in Image 2) feels uncomfortable right away. B is not interested in talking about tomorrow's weather, or about sports, and the economy is too depressing right now. B doesn't find any of those topics exciting or even interesting — not at a cocktail party.

Instead, B is interested in what lies beneath the surface. And I, of course, am B. I like to dive right into the ice-cold water and say: *"You know why I always talk to the people who are standing alone at cocktail parties? When I was 17, I went on a skiing trip — all by myself. I was young, and very shy, and I couldn't talk to anyone. I remember what an awful feeling it was, so today I like to talk to the people at a party who are standing all by themselves. Maybe they're lonely."*

And guess what? In little encounters like this, I've never had someone run away from me — no matter what you might have predicted. No, they usually will say something like: *"That's interesting — and don't we all get lonely sometimes? Actually, I remember ..."* And I've heard some very interesting stories — much more interesting than the next day's weather, or even the Superbowl.

You get the point. By refusing to be superficial, by being authentic and transparent, B rapidly gains the confidence of A, and something interesting can happen.

It's the same when you're speaking in public — you also have to dive into the water, even if at first it feels cold. Share anecdotes with the audience: stories about your problems with dating when you were younger, stories about your mistake of drinking and driving, stories about your idiosyncrasies, even stories about the loss of a loved one or about a broken marriage. The audience will hang on your every word. You'll be getting to them on an emotional level.

So, what are the limits to transparency? You set the limit. Set it high!

Be Jack Lemmon — be transparent!

STEP THREE
30 Seconds

Do you remember the cat who is so incredibly confident it can stand up to speak in front of 500 Rottweilers? Confidently the cat takes 500 leashes in its paw and pulls gently but firmly, creating a connective tension with the audience. When you speak in public, you have about 30 seconds, more or less, to create that tension between yourself and your listeners, to gain and hold their attention. Your very first sentence is the most crucial rhetorical tool you'll ever have — it's like the cat's paw, because you must use it to grab your audience's attention.

Boring George

You've heard of Curious George, but have you heard about Boring George? If we take a look at average speakers from all over the world — at congresses, banquets, seminars, fairs, weddings, or anywhere — we usually hear a standard, and boring, beginning:

"Hello everybody, and good evening! My name is George Boring, and it is a great honor and pleasure for me to have the opportunity tonight to talk to you about mobility in the 21st century..."

Is that a powerful beginning? If you were in the audience, would it grab your attention? Is this the powerful rhetoric that will blast all the way to the back row of a room filled with 500 guests who just had one too many glasses of red wine?

Let's take a closer look at this general, standard opening that we'll hear 99% of the time.

We Know You, George

George is already well known to us: his name appeared on the invitation, and again on the program, and if that weren't enough, somebody introduced him by name just a few moments ago. We know you, George! And we know what you're going to talk about, too, because that's on the invitation too, as well as on the agenda, and maybe on the sign outside the door as well. We know we're right in the middle of the evening, and we certainly know that it's a great honor and pleasure for you to be speaking to us — how could it be anything else? In short, you've been talking for almost a minute, but you haven't yet said anything we don't already know — so we're already half-way to falling asleep!

I've Never Sold A Car In My Life

Once, when I was with KPMG in Barcelona, I had to present the results of a market study whose objective was to analyze the various success factors for retail automobile sales in Spain. We'd invited seven top representatives of auto manufacturers, the country's biggest importer, and its biggest retailer, and a prominent professor of entrepreneurship, Pedro Nueno of IESE Business School. It was quite an exclusive group.

Had I been inspired by George Boring's standard beginning, I probably would have started my presentation like this:

"Hello everybody! I know it is early in the morning..." [Insert fake smile.] *My name is Florian Mueck, and I would like to share the results of our market study about success factors in automotive retail in Spain with you. Why don't we start right away by looking at ..."*

But I did not start like the other 99% of public speakers. Even then, I knew that the first sentence was my only chance, my 30-second chance, to wake everyone up — to grab the leashes of all those Rottweilers — and generate the tension necessary to keep their attention. So instead, I started like this:

"I've never sold a car in my life!" Here, instead of a fake smile, I paused for a full three seconds to let the audience think about what I'd just said. Then I continued: *"And I don't know whether any of you has ever sold a car in your lives, either."* I knew no one had — that much was certain. *"But* [pause], *after talking to all these actors in the marketplace* [theatri-

cally pointing at the first Powerpoint slide], *after listening to the needs and preoccupations of retailers, manufacturers, importers, dealerships, repair shops, financiers and customers, I can tell you one thing for sure: Selling a car must be one of the biggest challenges in our lives!"*

Professor Nueno would never have acknowledged my existence before I made that presentation, but ever since then, every time we see each other, he greets me with a big smile.

Be Creative

The first sentence is holy; it is sacred; it cannot be cluttered up with meaningless verbiage like *"Good evening"* or *"Hello everyone"* or *"My name is..."* An opening sentence must be catchy, a grabber — powerful.

Be creative. If you talk about water, drink a glass of water in one gulp first, then say: *"Water is great, but* [pause, and turn the empty glass upside-down] *there's not much left!"* If you're going to talk about music, sing! If you're speaking about the internet bubble of 2000, bring a balloon and let it explode, then say: *"I was a broker in New York, when the bubble burst!"*

Whatever you do, make it catchy and unexpected: ask a rhetorical question, for example, or simply exclaim in a single word: *"Divorce!"* — and let the pause be long enough to get a little uncomfortable. You could entertain the audience with body movements and nothing else. The list of possible openers is nearly infinite; it's only cut short by your imagination.

By the way, to obtain the greatest impact for your first sentence, make sure there is absolute silence in the room before you even open your mouth. Take your time; it can be difficult, but you must be patient. When the very last person has cleared his throat and his neighbor has stopped moving around on his chair, then you can uncork your magical intro and grab those Rottweilers by the leash.

Learn It By Heart

Since the first sentence is so extremely important to create tension between you and your audience, I strongly recommend that you write it
down and learn it by heart. You'll get a welcome side-benefit as well:
you won't have to think anymore about what to say at the beginning.

That's Better, George

So how could George have started his speech? Maybe with a quotation:

*"Enthusiasm is the yeast that makes your hopes shine to the stars. En-
thusiasm is the sparkle in your eyes, the swing in your gait. The grip of
your hand, the irresistible surge of will and energy to execute your ideas.
— Henry Ford's words seem timeless. Despite our crisis-battered sec-
tor, we are more enthusiastic than ever about what lies ahead. Hybrids,
electric cars, emission free cars — new challenges are reaching out to
everyone in this room. Let's face them with enthusiasm. Henry would be
proud of us!"*

When you start like this, you surprise the audience. Surprise means attention. Attention is what you want; attention is what you need.

*You have 30 seconds to grab those Rottweilers' leashes — be creative
and take your audience by surprise!*

STEP FOUR
Here's Looking At You, Kid

Doesn't it annoy you when speakers won't ever look at you? They might look at the ceiling, or just above everybody's head, but will never make direct eye contact with anyone. They could look at the floor, or off to the left when you're sitting on the right — it makes you feel left-out. *"Hey — look at me when you're talking to me,"* you might love to bark. You're the Rottweiler, and you're starting to think that cat's afraid of you, or at best, that it just doesn't care.

But what about yourself? I'm willing to bet that you would probably do exactly the same thing. Eye contact is difficult for most people. We feel somehow we are intruding, or making a challenge we don't mean to make. Just as our cerebellum tells us to avoid talking to strangers, it doesn't want us to be looking directly at strangers, either. We are socially programmed to avoid eye contact. It's a very complex matter, but basically, looking other people in the eye is a display of territorial dominance. In some cultures it's considered highly disrespectful, insolent or arrogant. You lose status in the stare-down contest if you're the first one to blink. When you're up in front of a crowd, you're literally vastly outnumbered, so the last thing you want to do is issue a territorial challenge.

Release The Hand Brake
That's all true, but it's just theory, too, and it comes from our distant past. Now, as a practical matter, you simply have to look into people's eyes — deeply! If you don't, they'll feel left out, even disrespected. And a part of them will know that you're afraid of them — which will make them disrespect you. But when you look into their eyes, you include them, make them feel important. And you show them you trust them enough not to be afraid of them — which means that they can trust you, too.

The ability to look someone in the eye is directly related to your own self-esteem. This brings us right back to the first step — confidence. It couldn't have been said more clearly than Maxwell Max said it: *"Low self-esteem is like driving through life with your hand brake on!"* You remember your first driving lessons — do you want to drive through life with your hand brake on? Of course not.

If you search Google for "eye contact AND public speaking" you will get a multitude of tips and tricks about how best to handle this delicate issue. One of the proposed methods is the figure-8 approach: your eyes follow an imaginary number eight over the room. Doing this lets you constantly cover the entire hall with your gaze.

My personal pattern is to choose three people in the audience, one in the front row on the left, one in the back in the center, and one in the front row on the right. Then I nonchalantly jump from one to another, from the left side to the center, from the center to the right, and back again. I keep my eyes moving — they should never linger anywhere more than a few seconds. This way, everyone in the audience feels part of your show; everyone feels involved and important.

Bridge Of Sympathy

Aside from addressing the audience generally, you can also use eye contact on an individual level. You could say, for example: *"Isn't it a tragedy that every day so many children have to starve to death in Africa?"* As you say that, you look directly at a woman in her mid-forties in the third row. There's a good chance she has children of her own. For sure, you will receive a confirming nod. You've just built a bridge of sympathy with that woman, and it will spread out through the rows like a pattern of falling dominos.

One trick I use whenever I can is to talk to a few people in the audience before the program gets started. (This isn't really a "trick," because it's something I enjoy doing anyway, but it is a good technique to remember.) By doing this, I gain what I call some "friendly faces." Then, during those few seconds when I'm waiting for the crowd to settle down before I unleash my opener, I make brief eye contact with them, just a quick nod or smile, and now I have people I can turn to in case the audience gets hostile, or in case I get a little nervous — and yes, I do still get nervous sometimes. My friendly faces are my anchors — they help me remember that there's nothing to be afraid of.

Keeping An Eye On Johnny

Finally, how many jokes about a little brat named Johnny have you heard? Now, think of your audience as a class. Odds are, there's at least one Johnny — that is, a potential troublemaker — and if you're a teacher, you'd better keep an eye on him. It's interesting that you'll almost always find Johnny in the back row — Johnnies like the back row. But if you look directly at Johnny frequently during your speech, he'll know you're watching him. And the best thing is, the last row never feels left out.

Look deep into their eyes. It makes them feel involved!

STEP FIVE
The Conqueror Of Fatigue

When was the last time you went skiing? Do you remember waiting at the ski lift waving at your friends and shouting: *"Hey, guys, here I am!"*

When was the last time you sat in a church during a wedding ceremony? Did you whisper into your neighbor's ear, making comments about the bride's wedding dress?

When was the last time you were sitting in a football stadium and yelled: *"Go, go, go!"*

When was the last time you were arguing with your partner at the supermarket, and you couldn't raise your voice because there were other people around?

You Already Know

Four examples. Four different types of voices. The great news is: you already know how to use your voice. You might not know how you produce sound, but certainly you can whisper, scream, shout, speak normally, and use a variety of different tones of voice.

Think about the last time you attended a party. You talked loudly; you even yelled: *"Where's the beer?"* You flirted; you talked softly; you put enthusiasm behind your words. You used your voice the way it should be used — with variety.

As the figure below sets out, you can talk slowly or fast, with a low voice or loudly. This offers you a variety of four basic combinations.

So my question is: Why do so many public speakers present their topic in such a monotonous tone of voice? And while I'm asking: Why do so many of them speak so softly?

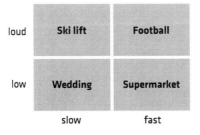

Don't you just hate it? It's bad enough that you're late and have to sit down in the last row, but then you find you can hardly hear what the speaker is saying! There's this mumbling going on up there, but you simply cannot make it out. So, what to do? Of course — play around with the free ballpoint pen, or pretend to be learning something from the handouts — or just sit there.

You Don't Yell At José Carreras

Good voice projection and good vocal variety are key to maintaining the tension and attention between yourself and your audience. I remember a keynote speech I gave in Barcelona, introducing an artist with a personalized address. It was the private preview of an exhibition in the lobby of a 5-star-hotel by the old harbor. The ceiling was quite high, maybe 50 feet, and the height and length of the room turned any raised voice into a vibrating echo, which is hardly a good situation for giving a speech. So I went straight to the manager to ask for the microphone, but he gave me this incredulous look and said, *"Sir, out of respect to our other hotel guests, you cannot use a microphone. I am very sorry."* Great! So it was me and my voice against a huge hall producing a giant echo, and 100 serious art lovers, among them José Carreras, the operatic tenor.

Times like these make me happy I've spent some of my spare time practicing my public speaking skills — especially my ability to project my voice. It went well because I know how to use my diaphragm to breathe. It's an easy enough technique[2] , mostly involving good posture, for those times when you have to speak loudly without yelling.

At other times, you can hold on to a larger group's full attention by speaking loudly sometimes, then speaking in a low voice. People will listen even more carefully then. Sometimes you can make your most significant points in a low voice. If you don't continue for very long, and provided your pronunciation and elocution are good, the audience will even be willing to strain a little bit, so they don't miss a single precious word you say.

---

[2] http://www.vocaltechnique.co.uk/breathing.html

It is, once again, all about practice and experience — and being willing to experiment.

The — — — Pause

Let's pay some special attention to Gandhi: his message of non-violent resistance had its greatest impact when he said nothing at all. It's the same when you're making a speech — sometimes what you need most is a little bit of silence. Mark Twain once said: *"The right word may be effective, but no word was ever as effective as a rightly timed pause."*

I touched on this in Step 3 — so let's think again about the opening sentence. In one of my seminars, Joel (a participant) volunteered to speak in a "get-to-the-point" exercise. He stood up straight, well balanced, firm, and waited for absolute silence. Then, in a clear, charismatic voice, he intoned: *"Divorce!"* One second — two seconds — three seconds. The people kept a terrified silence, anticipating. A brilliant beginning! Nothing he could have said during those 3 seconds would have been more powerful than his rhetorical pause after that evocative word: "divorce."

Pauses occur naturally, but too many speakers insist upon replacing them with "ah" or "um." Imagine how all those could be converted to pauses, and could create more suspense, more tension, instead of being distracting and annoying. But if everyone did the same thing, you wouldn't be special anymore, so let them continue with their ahs and ums. You are *The Seven Minute Star*: you pause — for effect. You can pause often — whenever you — want to.

You Are Not Boring

Knowing all this now — the powerful, variable voice you have, the impact you can cause by sometimes saying nothing — do something now: think about all those regular speakers again.

A monoooootonous voice is boooooooring!

You, however, are not boring! You share your excitement with the audience when, for instance, you talk about your experience of a parachute jump. You increase your speed when you're about to jump; you raise the volume; you almost yell, keeping it loud — you are falling — do not lower your voice yet, keep it going, let them be with you, take them with you. And then, BOOM, you pull the cord, you release the tension; your voice turns softer, more relaxed, calmer; you're looking out over the countryside. You feel so good.

The Conqueror Of Fatigue

With his famous kettledrum stroke, composer Joseph Haydn gave his symphony number 94, the "Surprise Symphony," such a sudden, unexpected, and above all noisy turn that it makes the entire audience wake up again. He did it on purpose, of course, after, again on purpose, almost lulling them to sleep. And although you don't want to put your audience to sleep the way Haydn did, you, the speaker, can also intersperse sudden changes in volume and speed. You can make your listeners feel like they're riding a rollercoaster — up and down, left and right. Your voice is not only there to be heard; your voice is the parachute; your voice is the rollercoaster; your voice conquers any possibility of audience fatigue.

Your voice is a sensitive beast — let it out of the cage!

STEP SIX
Mirror, Mirror On The Wall

The good news first: You do not have to be like Spencer Tracy in "Inherit the Wind" to be a great speaker! We also know that up to 80% of what and how we communicate is non-verbal[3]. This means you could emulate Buster Keaton, one of the best of the silent-movie era, whose mastery of body language is something you can learn as well. And it's one of the key success factors for keeping your audience's attention.

You Are Not A Clown

Most people think that overdoing their use of body language will cause the audience to perceive them as a clown.

Dear reader, let me set you straight about this: Not only are you not a clown — it would probably take you ten years to seem like a clown on stage.

Switch on your memory and go back to the last time you saw a series of presentations – a congress or a symposium. Now, who among all those nine speakers do you still remember? The answer is obvious – none! You probably don't remember a single one of them because they made no impact on you; they simply were not memorable. However, if you ever saw Benjamin Zander[4] , you'd remember him forever. His being an orchestra conductor (of the Boston Philharmonic) has, I'm certain, helped him learn to use body language so well. When he speaks publicly, his whole body expresses his enthusiasm. And he is not perceived as a clown at all; to the contrary, he is one of the most inspiring speakers out there.

One of the challenges we all face is that we usually don't know what we communicate non-verbally while we're speaking. Many books have been written on this subject; this is not another one; however, I will quickly touch a few important points.

Move Before You Say It

Imagine yourself making a presentation, and you're going to say: *"Stop!"* Before you say it, put your hand up in the "stop" gesture, palm out. With a one second delay, say: *"Stop!"* Now imagine doing exactly the same

---

[3] http://edo.med.miami.edu   [4] http://www.benjaminzander.com

thing, but in reverse order: first say *"Stop!"* then hold your palm out. It seems like such a small difference, but the impact is much greater when we move our bodies first, and then say what we're going to say.

As another example: yell: *"Enough!"* Then bang your fist on the table. And you know what comes next: first bang your fist on the table, wait for one second — while you look fiercely into the eyes of an imaginary audience — then cry out: *"Enough!"*

Another example: draw a bridge in the air in front of you with your hand. At the peak, say: *"The bridge of happiness..."* — pause — then finish drawing the bridge, *"...has always connected us!"*

You get the point. If you speak first and move afterwards, you throw as much as 80% of the communicative impact right out the window and into the trash can. To put it positively: you'll gain up to 80% more impact when you move your body first.

Mirrors Are Everywhere

I said that we usually can't really know how other people perceive our body language, but I've found an easy way around the problem. I simply use mirrors. They really are everywhere — in bathrooms, in elevators, in cars, in hallways. And windows often make imperfect but useful mirrors. They're everywhere. You do want to make sure, though, that you're not perfecting a Jim Carrey pose where your boss could come in and catch you doing it.

When I recommend this in my seminars, the participants usually roll on the floor laughing. But I don't really see what's so funny. I want to know the way my body speaks. Once I know that, I can use it to emphasize my message and purposefully evoke emotional reactions in the audience such as sadness, sympathy, disgust, joy or happiness. Have you ever been in a dance studio? Talk about body language — dancing is nothing else. There aren't any walls there — only mirrors. When dancers practice, they absolutely have to know what they look like. Mirrors are great for practicing — and they're free.

Tear Down This Wall

Let's have another picnic with our cerebellum — an idea Hannibal Lecter would appreciate. Our instincts reside in our cerebellum. We cannot cheat them, and we surely cannot run away from them. Instinctive behavior has been encoded into us over millions of years.

It's crucial for speakers, that the audience trust them about what they're saying. And the band of trust is delicate. We all know that. We look for the mistake, not for the ingenuity. We envy more than we admire. We are more suspicious than trustful — especially with strangers, and as a speaker, you are normally the stranger in the room.

What factors influence trust? Credibility, of course, and reliability, a lack of self-interest, the ability to create a feeling of intimacy. And there is another extremely important factor that generates trust: transparency.

Whatever you may think about George W. Bush, in terms of body language and transparency, his handshake is legendary. He slightly bends toward the other person, reaches out his hand and, turning it at a 45° angle, he spreads his fingers wide open. This sends out a signal of full transparency. The other person's cerebellum says: *"This guy is fully exposed, naked; he doesn't hide anything; he can be trusted; keep talking to him!"*

Now take a look at your arms and your hands in relation to your body. When you speak in public, do you hide one or both of your hands in your pockets? Do you hide your arms behind your body? Do you hide your body behind the lectern?

You must tear down the walls, the protections you put around yourself when you're up there in front of an audience. Show your hands! Keep your arms out in front of you! Turn the laptop slightly and step aside instead of staying behind the lectern. When there's a table in front of you, don't lean against it; step back, or, what's even better, go around in front of it. Never show your back to the audience. Be transparent at all times!

No Seated Speeches

In panel discussions, usually several speakers sit at a long table on stage. One after another gives a speech — while staying seated! Another wall — tear it down! Stand up when you speak. It conveys more confidence, more transparency. Never forget: they want to look up to you.

If you have no choice, you have to live with it. There are round panel discussions set among tables, sofas or chairs. But as soon as the moderator grants you five minutes and asks you to sum up your professional career, or your topic, or to give your opinion about the theme of the day, grab hold of your chance — stand up. It doesn't matter if the others don't — or, rather, it does matter, because your opinion will be delivered more effectively than the others, and get a better reception.

Search For Feedback

One of the most common ways we sabotage ourselves is in making our self-assessment. All of us tend to see ourselves either better or certainly different, from the way others perceive us. As the poet said:

Oh would some power the gift give us
To see ourselves as others see us!
It would from many a blunder free us,
And foolish notion.[5]

Especially when it comes to your non-verbal communication, my advice is to ask your family and your friends to help you practice and give you their honest feedback. You'll find that it's very valuable most of the time. When you're learning public speaking, any constructive criticism will take you to a higher level.

Maybe You Will Become Spencer Tracy

Like a monotonous voice, a monotonous gaze, posture, and stance will destroy the rapport between you and the audience that you worked hard

---

[5] Robert Burns, "To A Louse" (dialect edited)

to establish with your opening sentence. Train yourself. Practice your different facial expressions — your smile, your frown, your embarrassed or skeptical looks. Your body already contains a limitless repertoire of expressions. Explore them, use them. Who knows? You might actually turn into an actor. It's all about your audience's long term memory, and about being remembered. You can be the one out of nine speakers at that congress who'll be remembered. Be an actor, and persuade your audience the way Spencer Tracy got the people up on their feet, cheering.

You are not a clown! Your body speaks wonderfully. Let it talk!

STEP SEVEN
They Are Everywhere

Consider Steve Jobs and his legendary product-launch presentations. Imagine him presenting his revolutionary inventions empty handed! No iPad; no iPhone; no iPod; no iBook! The presentations, and the world, would have been completely different. Or try to imagine Columbus telling his egg[6] story without using an egg.

The World Is Avatar

Visual aids – props — make any speech more memorable. We all stick to our Powerpoints, fine, well and good, but a Powerpoint slide is (for the time being, at least) two-dimensional. Human beings see the world in three dimensions. Consider James Cameron's blockbuster "Avatar" — it's just the first — they're all going for 3-D eventually.

Visual aids are tangible anchor points for the audience. They connect what you say with an object you display. Once I held up a tube of instant glue and said: *"In the end, not even this superglue could keep our relationship together."* Consider trying to say this without using the prop — it just wouldn't work.

Even A Mirror Is A Visual Aid

Another piece of good news: Just like mirrors, visual aids are everywhere. And a mirror can even be a visual aid. I remember addressing the American Society of Barcelona at Thanksgiving dinner. I was telling them: *"Somewhere on our path from innocent childhood to the adult world of realism, we lose our smile. At some point we let it drop like a hot potato"* — and I let drop a real hot potato. I continued: *"We have to rediscover our smiles! But where to look for them? This morning while I was taking a shower, I had an idea. A mirror! Why not? A mirror might be a great place to rediscover your smile. And by coincidence I have one with me!"*

I went up to an important-looking gentleman and held the mirror right in front of his face. *"Sir, can you see your smile?"* He was a bit puzzled,

[6] Columbus' egg: A popular story about how a brilliant idea or discovery seems simple or easy after the fact. Christopher Columbus, having been told that discovering the Americas was no great accomplishment, challenged his critics to make an egg stand on its tip; after they gave up, he did it himself by tapping the egg on the table so as to flatten its tip. (Source: Wikipedia.org)

but he gamely tried to put on his best smile. I commented: *"Well, I think you can do better than this!"* Everyone laughed. Next I approached a rather introverted lady sitting in the farthest corner of the room. She gave me such an innocent, touching smile that I exclaimed, *"Congratulations, ladies and gentlemen, we've just rediscovered our smiles!"* Of that entire speech, the audience loved the mirror part most. It was an interactive visual prop that made people laugh and feel great. It was priceless.

Visual aids are everywhere.
* Your cell phone. When you say, *"I called my friend and he said, ..."* take out your cell phone and pretend that you're talking to your friend.
* When you say, *"I'm an American!"* hold up your passport just a split second before.
* Put on a pair of shades when you say, *"What an incredible long night of negotiations. The next day I looked like a Zombie!"*
* Use a piggybank when you're discussing the problem of too much household savings.
* Use a half-full glass of water when you talk about positivity.
* Pull out a Mont-Blanc pen when you point out that, in the good old days, we used to sign letters with ink, not with a J-Peg.

"Have you seen this morning's paper?" I don't even need to tell you what to show with this question. Visual aids are everywhere.

Always One — But Never More Than Three
There is no hard-and-fast rule about using visual aids, but my personal experience tells me, you should always use at least one prop, but never use more than three.

Why no more than three? Your speech has a flow to it, a rhythm. When you use your props smoothly, they have the greatest impact. But it's also true that, when you set something up, or unwrap it, or position or post it — whatever you have to do with it, if no more than to look for it and pick it up — it causes a short interruption of your flow. If you use the A-B-C speech structure (Step 8), I recommend that you use one visual aid for each of the three main parts of your speech body.

The Visual Aid Of Powerpoint?

These days, a presentation without Powerpoint is like apple pie without cheese. Powerpoint has become a ubiquitous tool in the world of business presentations. Of course Powerpoint serves as a visual aid, but you should use only full-screen images to achieve the best effect. Quoting Gandhi and showing a huge image of the Hindu leader is just perfect.

Use metaphoric images to support your message! If you talk about clean energy, project an image of the rainforest up on the wall. If you talk about teamwork, you could use the image of leafcutter ants building an ant-bridge to help their "teammates."

Always ask yourself: Do I want the audience to read, or do I want them to listen? Avoid mixing images and text on a Powerpoint slide if at all possible — using both distracts an audience. Their attention should be on you, not on the text. They can't listen to you and read at the same time. If you feel you do need some words, take a suggestion from Garr Reynolds[7] , a renowned blogger on public speaking: Use only a few words. Then it's like a punch line.

I like to use an image of a spider (A) in my presentation about networking. First I show only the image, and I ask: *"When do you think this spider works on her web?"* Some good answers I've heard are: *"In the morning!"* or *"When it's broken!"* Then someone will exclaim: *"Always!"* — and that's the moment I click the remote, and the image with the punch line (B) appears.

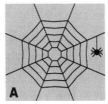 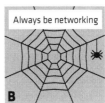

[7] http://www.presentationzen.com

Always remember that you're the cat up in front of 500 Rottweilers. You have to keep a firm grip on their leashes. Don't make any move, like letting them read, that lets them think they could slip the leash and get away from you.

Involve The Audience

There was another time I wanted to use the mirror as a prop, but I'd arrived there late, and didn't have time to get hold of one. When I got to the part about the mirror, I had to wing it, so, spontaneously, I approached the audience, and said: *"We men — we've never really understood what exactly it all is that you ladies carry around in those bags. But there are three things I believe all of you have in there — a lipstick, Kleenex and a mirror! May I ask the ladies in this room — would one of you please lend me a mirror for a moment?"* Of course I got one right away.

What You Wear Is What We See

Speakers often ask themselves what they should wear when they're about to go on stage. A suit and shirt, with or without a tie, will always be fine. But, depending on the seriousness of the occasion, your clothing itself could also serve as a visual aid. Once my friend Melinda from Curaçao spoke about her passion for diving. She entered the room wearing her complete diving outfit, including her fins. It was truly amazing, and she had the audience completely on her side. But it all depends on both the occasion and the purpose of the speech.

Your Creativity Has No Limits

There's no limit to how creative you can be with your visual aids. Surprise your audience; they'll always be impressed. And if you've shown them a book that's about the topic of your speech, that's great too — pass it around at the end of your talk, so people can touch it, see it, and feel it. They'll feel more connected to a part of your speech, and to you. Congratulations!

The world is "Avatar." Follow Cameron's example: impress your
audience in three dimensions!

STEP EIGHT
No Parthenon

A typical situation: The medical professor has apparently finished his 87-slide presentation when he lets fly with that horrendous statement: *"Before I forget, I also wanted to point out that..."*

Speakers often try to tell their audience everything they know about their topic, but audiences are happy with anything new or interesting they can learn from you. They don't know what you know, so you don't need to tell them everything.

Get To The Point

Less is more. That's a fundamental rule of public speaking. For their first exercise, I ask my seminar participants to present their life in three minutes. In most cases, they're about to enter university when their time is up. We may be afraid to talk at first, but once we get going, the time simply whizzes by. We need a structure that will help us get to the point.

The optimal speech structure consists of an introduction, a body with three parts — A, B, C — and a closing. Let's focus first on the A-B-C. How do we get to the point?

Any topic provides a multitude of facets to cover. Think about your own life. Try making some brief notes on a sheet of paper about the most exciting aspects of your life, anecdotes, incidents, anything you think would capture the attention of an audience: your military service, your unforgettable trip to Bali, your first love, your student exchange experience in Barcelona, your passion for basketball, your dusty clarinet, your addiction to networking — whatever you want to mention.

Once you've reduced your life to some catchy phrases, draw a circle around the three that are the most striking. Within two minutes, you have your A-B-C. The same procedure works just fine with any topic you can think of, from quantum physics to Oktoberfest, from market study results to the homecoming dance, an image presentation of tomorrow's new car, or fertility rituals in ancient Greece.

But getting back to your own life: *"I was born in Dallas on June 25 1968..."* No! That fact would only be interesting if something else happened on that day — like July 20, 1969, the day of the first moon landing — something memorable like that. The audience doesn't want to hear what's on your resume — but this is how most people would present their lives. The audience would much rather hear about your dusty old clarinet, which helped you get through your time in the military because you played it in the marching band, because you entertained everybody with it at student parties, because you won the love of your life with it when you played "As Time Goes By" for her. Three themes, each one easy to understand, tied together with one thread. It touches people's emotions. It's awesome! Forget the resume.

The Speech Structure Building

If your speech were structured like a building, you could build the Empire State Building, the Eiffel Tower or the Guggenheim Museum. I like to use a Greek temple with three columns; it always serves me well; I've never yet encountered a speech topic for which I couldn't use this structure.

The foundation of your speech is the first sentence (Step 3), which introduces your topic. And remember: you have only 30 seconds to grab those Rottweilers' leashes. Build a catchy, surprising, different foundation. Imagine it was designed by Salvador Dalí or Frank Lloyd Wright.

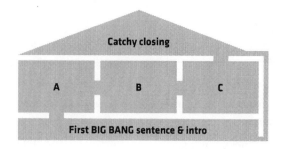

You have just learned how to put your A-B-C points together. These build the main body that stands on top of your base. Three points have the most impact. You can use up to five, but don't build a Parthenon; keep it short; be a minimalist!

On top of your pillars is the roof, the closing. I like to make sure there's a drain-pipe going down from the roof — to let water flow back to the foundation. Or think of it as coming *full circle*, or *the umbrella effect* — something that connects the end back to the beginning, to round off the picture.

Suppose you start your speech with a quotation: *"Charlie Chaplin once said: 'A day without a smile is a lost one.'"* Since he composed the theme song to the 1936 classic "Modern Times," you could round off your speech by singing: *"Smile when your heart is aching..."* Don't be scared — you don't have to be a karaoke star to be a great speaker, or even to sing a little bit sometime during your speech. This is just to give you some ideas.

Or, getting more down to earth, you could begin your speech by asking, *"Have you been to Africa? I haven't, unfortunately, but what I heard about child soldiers is really shocking!"* Your closing then could be something like: *"If all we do is talk about changing the world, we'll never change it for the better. That's why I've decided to volunteer as an aid-worker in Sierra Leone and take an active part as an agent of change in the world!"*

A-B-C, Not A-C-B

When you've nailed down the three main points for the body of your speech, it's time to put them in order. You could move from the least to the most significant, from the oldest to the newest, from past to future, from small to large. What's important is that the order of A-B-C have a logic to it, that the movement you choose makes some sort of sense.

Smooth, Clear Transitions

Too often I've heard a Toastmasters evaluator tell a speaker: *"You had a structure in your speech, but it was difficult for us in the audience to follow it. We never knew when one topic ended or when the next one started. We got lost."*

Your speech has four key transitions, and it's important to focus on them. The first comes right after your introduction. You might say, *"I will share three facets of my life with you that had a major impact on who I am today!"* Just before you say that, you hold up three fingers. Then you can keep using your fingers to the audience through your content, the body of your speech: first, second, third, A-B-C. The last transition connects your third point, C, with the closing: *"As I said at the beginning ..."*

One simple but effective idea I've used is to show sheets of A4 paper with the titles printed on them as I started each separate point. I paused, I kept silent, as I held up each sheet of paper, and the audience loved these effective little breaks.

Again, I invite you to be creative. Let your thoughts take a few wild turns. There are no rules in public speaking. You create your own rules. ***You are The Seven Minute Star!***

20-60-20

The A-B-C structure is most effective if you follow a simple timing guideline. Use 20% of your time for the introduction, 60% for the body of your speech, and 20% for the closing. If you have five minutes for your speech, that's a 1 minute intro, 3 minutes for your A-B-C points, and 1 minute for the closing.

Why Seven Minutes?

When you put all of this book's 15 steps into practice, you should be able to talk for an hour without being boring. But it's only common sense that short speeches are better than longer ones — they're sharper, they get right to the point, and they're usually more entertaining. I've always thought that the Toastmasters 5 to 7 minute time-frame is just perfect.

Help comes sometimes from the most unexpected places. When I told my friend Sinan about *The Seven Minute Star*, he revealed to me an insight of his as a marketing consultant for conferences and fairs — the preferred duration of speeches will gravitate towards 7 minutes in the future: *"You can keep the tension for about seven minutes. After that people will start to leave the room. When the speeches are seven minutes long, attendees tend to stay and wait for more speeches."*

If you're facing a 45 minute time-slot or even more for your presentation, please send me an email to florian@thesevenminutestar.com and we'll figure out how you can do it!

Please — No 'Thank You'

When you conclude your speech, please stay away from one of my pet peeves. Speakers almost always say *"Thank you!"* at the end. But remember: You are *The Seven Minute Star*! Shouldn't the audience be thanking you for your inspiring performance? Don't worry about being perceived as arrogant when you close without saying *"Thank you."* Leaving it out actually emphasizes the final point you've made, while using it detracts from that point — and, I would argue, from your entire speech!

Consider this conclusion: *"In my entire life I will never forget standing in that dark room in Yad Vashem, the Holocaust Museum of Jerusalem. In the center, six eternal flames, the walls of the room made up of a never-ending number of mirrors at diverse angles. There were only six flames in that room, but what I saw was an infinite number of light dots reaching into eternity, and I knew that each and every single one of them reflected the loss of one human life. This incredible experience will follow me until my very last day…. Thank you!"* Do you see what I mean? You'd simply be smothering those powerful emotional vibes you spent so much effort to create if you say *"Thank you"* at the end. Why would you want to do that? Can you imagine Hannibal Lecter saying: *"Clarice, have the lambs stopped screaming? Thank you!"*

Please, please don't say *"Thank you."* Say what you have to say, then take a half-step back. That's it; that's all you need to do. The audience will know it's the end, and the first movement in the crowd will be applause.

***Construct your own speech structure building in less than five minutes. It works with any speech!* ***

STEP NINE
Cicero, Demosthenes, & Co.

You can do the greatest show on earth on stage and you still may not be *The Seven Minute Star.* No speech is great without great content! But what is great content? First, you have to consider the context. You can bring up the best speech with the greatest content about how smoking increases your personal quality of life, but if you do that in front of the Against Lung Cancer Association, the crowd will most likely tear you apart!

Another observation: art is subjective. Some people think the circles and lines in a Joan Miró painting are nothing more than circles and lines; others see them as a minimalist masterpiece. The same thing applies to the content of your speech. For some it might be too explicit, while others might find it funny. Some might think it's dull, but others would say it fit perfectly with the complexity of your topic. Some may dislike or even detest the humorous parts of your speech, while others might just love them.

The art of choosing your content is always to aim for the majority of the audience. Those are the ones you want to engage, like a politician who aims at the political center to attract the highest number of voters. And give the people rhetorical lighthouses that will stand out of the grey fog of content; it will make them love your speech even more. I've listed a few of them below.

Yes, We Can
John F. Kennedy, Gandhi, Martin Luther King, Winston Churchill, Tony Robbins — these are the most common names my seminar attendees come up with when I ask them to name some of the great, charismatic public speakers of our time. When you talk about the all-time greats, though, the names of the Roman Cicero and the Greek Demosthenes will always come up. Many famous speakers over the centuries have emulated them.

But the one mentioned most often nowadays is Barack Obama. Thanks to his twittered and facebooked presidential campaign of 2008,

Obama has climbed the Mount Olympus of public speaking. His triumphal, hopeful outcry, *"Yes, we can!"* mobilized millions. He repeated it over and over again. One secret of the art of rhetoric lies in repetition. You just have to say something often enough, and even though people might not believe you, they will certainly start listening to your message. Just think about "weapons of mass destruction" — it became so familiar, now we only need to say "WMDs."

Politicians are generally great at repeating their message over and over, and you too can take advantage of this technique by repeatedly using their assertions, *"We have always told you..."* or *"We have initiated..."* The good thing about that latter statement is that, even if you've never finished anything, you'll always sound so full of initiative. What a great guy you must be!

Boom, Boom, Becker

Bild (engl. image) is Germany's biggest tabloid. Bild is famous for its sensational front-page headlines, all in capital letters of course. One of its most memorable headlines delighted the German people in 1985: "BOOM, BOOM, BECKER" Boris Becker, only 17 years old, had just won Wimbledon.

Tabloids use rhetorical devices all the time, and in only three words, "BOOM, BOOM, BECKER," Bild used three of them. Onomatopoeia refers to words that imitate the sounds, objects, or actions they refer to: 'BOOM'. Anaphora is a succession of phrases or sentences beginning with the same word or group of words: 'BOOM, BOOM.' Alliteration is a succession of words that begin with the same sound, and in most cases the same letter: the 'B' of 'BOOM' and 'BECKER.'

So when you write your speech, make sure you include something that reverberates, like 'Boom, Boom, Becker' or "Veni, Vidi, Vici."[8] These things stick in an audience's memory like a great song or a highly-charged, chiming chant.

---

[8] "Veni, vidi, vici": a famous sentence in Classical Latin reportedly written by Julius Caesar in 47 BC as a summary report of his short war with Pharnaces II of Pontus. It means: "I came, I saw, I conquered." Its form (a three-part sentence or motto) is classed as a tricolon and a hendiatris. Source: Wikipedia.org

Another Bridge Of Sympathy

Christian Angele from Berlin-based imedo.de was an enthusiastic participant in my seminar. I loved his feedback on how I could have built an even better "bridge of sympathy" between myself and the group. The bridge of sympathy is a great metaphor to describe what you as a public speaker should always make your top priority: to make the audience feel that you are one of them, that you understand their feelings, their needs, their worries, their visions, and their dreams.

How can you build that bridge of sympathy? Sympathy is all about sharing emotions and feelings, resonating with each other. Think of some beautiful and some horrible events in your life, things that others in the audience will have experienced as well:

- *"I remember my first kiss..."*
- *"It was a terrible, terrible moment when my brother sent me a text message with the first lines of Mozart's Requiem. He just couldn't call me to tell me that our Daddy had just passed away."*
- *"I never really get along with my boss..."*
- *"They say it's the happiest day of your life. Maybe it's true, but I also was so tired all day long!"*
- *"It was only by coincidence that I was the first to arrive at the scene where my best friend Oliver had his deadly accident. I really do hope that none of you has to go through such a moment of absolute horror."*
- *"For some of us, childhood is a chapter better left unwritten. I was fortunate. I would buy that book ten times."*

When you deliver messages like these, you evoke positive or negative emotions from the audience. You'll receive many confirming nods, because we all have fathers, we all have mothers, we all have best friends, we all have loved ones, and alas, we all have lost loved ones.

Build these bridges of sympathy into your speech. The audience might not remember what you said, but they will say: *"I kind of like that guy!"*

BRIDGES OF SYMPATHY

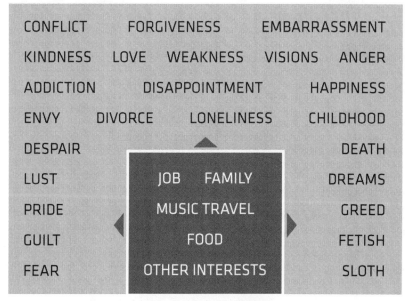

CONFLICT   FORGIVENESS   EMBARRASSMENT

KINDNESS   LOVE   WEAKNESS   VISIONS   ANGER

ADDICTION   DISAPPOINTMENT   HAPPINESS

ENVY   DIVORCE   LONELINESS   CHILDHOOD

DESPAIR   DEATH

LUST   JOB   FAMILY   DREAMS

PRIDE   MUSIC TRAVEL   GREED

GUILT   FOOD   FETISH

FEAR   OTHER INTERESTS   SLOTH

STANDARD TOPICS

Don't You Agree That...

...we all work too much? Of course, we can all agree on that! A rhetorical question is another structural piece you can use when you're designing the building that is your speech. They make great signals about your content. They can also be effective opening lines: *"Do you believe me when I tell you that, in only seven minutes, I will inspire you today to become a better person?"* You'll probably see a lot of "How should I know?" looks on their faces. But you exude conviction with your whole body and your voice from the moment you begin speaking, so you've got them thinking about a potential answer, and you've definitely captured their attention.

Anchor Of Attraction

Metaphors are lovely and useful friends of any speech writer. They touch
the different senses of your audience, and turn complex issues into tangible, easy-to-understand images:

- *"Whoever cut off the root of hope that this company would one day
  rise again — he must have been a lousy gardener!"*
- *"The walls of freedom are hard to climb for those who believe that
  some day a door to walk through will simply appear."*
- *"The anchor of attraction of this brand cannot be found on the floor
  of the sea, but in the heart of our passionate team!"*
- *"Some out there say our fire of passion for this company has been
  extinguished. But I see that flame. You see that flame. That flame
  is growing bigger every day. Let us show them that our fire of passion for this company was burning, is still burning, and will always
  be burning!"*

Once again I'd like to address your creative side. You might think that
using metaphors when you're presenting your business unit's monthly
results is a bit above and beyond — but I could not disagree more. Public
speaking happens anywhere and everywhere and all the time. You can
apply any of these methods to any situation — you can even pimp up the
way you talk about your monthly results: *"The financial milestones we
set for this year have turned out to be too heavy for this shaky ground
we're standing on thanks to the global financial crisis!"* Why not? People will remember — and when it comes time for a promotion, they'll
think of you.

The KPMG Soccer Team

Since metaphors add such vivid richness to the content of your speech,
here is another example.

For 3,013 days I worked for KPMG, a global professional services firm, first in Germany, then in Spain. During my time in Spain I had various opportunities to present the company. The problem for me was that KPMG, one of the Big 4, is quite a conservative turf to plant commercial seed. It makes me shiver even to think about these bullet points of its organizational structure:

- 100 partners
- 500 managers
- 1400 staff

You can present the same content in a more exciting way based on a single metaphor: *"For twenty years I've been playing soccer. Since the day I entered KPMG, I always thought this organization was like a soccer team. There's the goalie — nobody really pays attention to him, everyone takes him for granted, but when he's needed, everyone expects him to be there and be ready. That's the administration. There's the defense — technically it's not so advanced; they try their best to improve, they practice a lot, and get paid less than anyone else. That's the staff. There's the midfield — they run more than anybody else; they have to help the defense, plus make passes to the strikers, and sometimes they have to score a goal themselves. Poor guys — they're the managers. And the strikers? They have the most fame, the most money. You may not even see them for 89 minutes, but when the decisive moment comes, there they are, with the knowledge, experience, and instinct to score the important goals. Clearly, that's the partners."* By the way, the slide with the three bullet points now shows some soccer action, so it's much better, more interesting and fun. Anything is possible. Just be creative!

The Niche Guys

Before I suggested that you always focus on the majority opinion in the audience. True, but you can also try to get the niche guys involved. A trick I often use is to expand into the field of political incorrectness, then quickly retreat. I might say, for example, *"Those who touch the ground of political incorrectness today are banished, so I won't touch it. If I did,*

though, I'd say something about sexual harassment of men at work."
This approach is the rhetorical device called *paralipsis*: you tell the audience just exactly what it is that you're not even going to discuss. The
Roman orator Cicero was famous for using this device against his political enemies. It allows you to mention the unmentionable without com-
mitting to it.

Inform, Persuade, Motivate, Inspire, Entertain

People are always asking me about the message of a speech. Isn't the
message important as well? Of course it is, but it's important to understand that what drives your message is not the content itself, but the
purpose of giving the speech.

There are four basic purposes of a speech: to inform, to persuade,
to motivate, and to inspire. You'll adapt your message to the purpose of
your speech.

If you want to inform your audience, you must make sure you either
know your topic very well, or you must research your topic even better.
Informative speeches are usually rather dry, even boring; they're the
most difficult type of speech to make entertaining, even if your audience
is keen on learning something new, or on understanding a complex issue.
Your message is the content itself.

Persuasive speeches are different. If, for example, you want to persuade people to vote for a different political party, you have to give them
first class arguments. What's in it for them if they do as you say? *"This
is better because..."* — no, don't say that. It's lame; it would never persuade a hostile audience. People will defend their convictions the way
Braveheart defended Scotland. Instead, sell them a dream, something
they'd love to have but can't — under the current regime.

Or imagine trying to persuade a group of alcoholics to stop drinking. You wouldn't say, *"Stop drinking, it is bad for you!"* Your success
rate would be a big, fat zero. Instead, you might explain, in the brightest
words, how wonderful the feeling is when you cross the line after you've

run 26 miles 385 yards and successfully accomplished your first New York marathon. Then, almost as an afterthought, your message: *"Oh, and I forgot to mention — drinking alcohol and running marathons don't really go together!"*

A motivational speech is meant to make the audience take action. *"Do more sports!"* would be a classic topic. Authenticity is paramount. If you are overweight yourself, don't tell people to do more sports — talk about something else. However, no one would have more credibility than Lance Armstrong for encouraging people who suffer from a severe disease to stay strong, never give up, and believe in the impossible. He won the Tour de France, the most demanding bicycle race in the world, after beating cancer. Lance can say: *"I did it, you can do it! Go out there, do sports, eat right, and always keep your goal in mind! You can do it!"* I'd believe him; I'd take action today.

The king of speeches for me is the inspirational speech. You don't inform people. You don't try to persuade them. You don't want them to take any particular action. You do want to accomplish an even higher goal — you want to get them to change their attitude! When you give an inspirational speech, it isn't enough to be authentic. You must also be a role model. Barack Obama didn't try to persuade the American people to vote for the Democrats. He inspired them to believe in change, and the American people believed in him. To change a behemoth like the American establishment, you need immense amounts of enthusiasm and perseverance. Barack's campaign made him a symbol for both of these qualities. His speeches were simply inspiring!

Finally, I'm sure you've noticed that I didn't include entertainment as a possible purpose for a speech. That's because entertainment should be inherent in any speech. Apart from stand-up comedy there's really no such thing as pure entertainment. Any speech is going to have one of the four purposes I've talked about. But any and all of them can be entertaining. And, I guarantee that if you follow all the 15 steps I'm laying out for you, you'll entertain your audience every time.

How To Prepare Your Content

You've prepared a well-written speech; you've learned it by heart, you stand up to speak, only to find that — you're nervous — and you've forgotten your carefully-written text. Well — I'm here to tell you, this doesn't need to happen ever again. There's a better way!

Using notes in public speaking is like wearing earmuffs. You can wear them, but they'll never look good on you!

I suggest you write down the first and your last sentences of your speech and learn them by heart, word for word. These two sentences have to be perfect, because the audience's first impression, and their last impression, are the two most important factors in how they perceive you.

To the body of your speech, the A-B-C, you should only write out your bullet points — highlighting key points, and particular expressions you want to use.

Once you have these things down on paper, it's all about rehearsing, rehearsing, rehearsing. The Greek orator Demosthenes is legendary for practicing his speeches rigorously. Mirrors, partners, and friends are all great test audiences!

If you cannot live without your earmuffs, you might use your speech structure building (Step 8). Type in the main points and print it out on half an 8½ x 11 page — which you should have laminated, to give it a more professional look.

Ready — set — go!

Your show makes you a prince, but content is king! Learn from Cicero, Demosthenes, & Co. and sharpen your rhetorical weapons!

STEP TEN
Whiskeymill

Do you remember your Grandma telling you stories before you fell asleep? Have you ever asked yourself why the tabloid press is so successful? Why do you laugh so much with the stars of stand-up comedy?

The secret ingredient is — story-telling. Whether we listen to the fairytales our Grandma told us, or the latest flashmob attack on Oprah Winfrey, or everyday situations as seen through the eyes of a comedian like Jerry Seinfeld — we all love to hear stories.

When you share personal anecdotes with the audience, you allow yourself to become more personal to them. As you tell it, the audience will hear your story and relate it to their own experience, identifying their experience with yours, building another robust sympathetic bridge.

Everyday Situations

I love to meet new people. A plane, for instance, is always a great place for that. But we also know that sometimes, after a hard day of work, the last thing you want to have next to you on your trip from New York to L.A. is a guy who talks at you like Eddie Murphy in "48 Hours." So the first thing I ask my neighbor, when I sit down in a plane, is, *"Are you a reader or a talker?"*

Everybody in the audience will have been on a plane, so what you'll find is that some people in the audience will be readers, the kind who prefer to be left alone. Others will be talkers, people who'd love to talk, but sometimes are frustrated by a neighbor who wants to read, sleep, or just be left alone. But you've addressed both types of people, so everyone will end up laughing at your story; all of them can identify with it. So look for chances to mention everyday situations that fit with your speech, and tell them in your own words, based on your own experience.

Childhood Stories

Whether you had a good childhood or not so good, we were all young once. When you share anecdotes from your own childhood, especially the more significant memories, it can be like piercing right into an emotional hornets' nest.

Any time I touch on the subject of loneliness, I bring up my trip to Turin: *"I was 14 years old, and our soccer team took a trip. It had been all fun, until I made an offhand comment I thought was no big deal. I told my friend, who was half German, half Italian, that his parents made a 'weird-looking' couple. Stefan didn't take it as no big deal or an offhand remark, and what followed was the most difficult lesson I learned in my entire childhood. After what I'd thought was just an innocent remark, no one would talk to me any more — and I didn't understand. Then another guy on the team — much bigger than I was — decided he wanted to start a fight with me. No one would share a bedroom with me, either — I was by myself in a room with seven empty beds, and yelling and even threats were coming at me from the other side of the door: 'Mueck, we're going to get you!' they shouted. I was in an agony of panic. I put a pile of books up against the door, and managed to survive the night, but for the next few days no one would talk to me. They urged the coach to kick me off the team; everyone was against me. What it taught me was to persevere — I refused to give up. I fought for Stefan's friendship, and a few months later he did become my best friend, so the story came out all right. But I'll never forget that empty feeling I had, and I certainly learned never to disrespect people any more."*

We've all had moments when we've felt lost and alone, and we've all had to learn to persevere in the face of a bad situation. So talk about these things, about the emotional lessons you've learned; use your own experiences to express yourself. Always keep in mind that you'll be more effective if you build those bridges of sympathy.

Experience Vs. Theory

Imagine you were presenting the results of a market study to some 80 marketers. You must of course discuss the survey method. You could try to convince the audience that, for one or another statistical reason, a written survey would give you more accurate results for that specific project than a phone survey would. Or, you could say: *"How many of you have ever conducted a telephone survey? I have! Once I had to call 800 medium-sized German industrial companies to get their insights about best practices in facility management. Could it have been any worse? Three weeks later, I was three years older! And guess what? Ever since that fateful moment, I've always used written surveys."* You wind up transmitting exactly the same message, but your own personal experience is far more interesting than some gray theoretical analysis of data-collection methods.

So share your personal and professional experiences with your audience — they can certainly work to spice up the necessary theoretical parts!

Whiskeymill
You remember Step 2 when you were diving into ice-cold water? Networking is always a good topic, because everyone needs a network. When I want to explain how I make contacts at cocktail parties or congresses, I unwrap the anecdote of the Whiskeymill. *"I was 17 when my parents sent me all alone on a four-day skiing trip to Söll, in Austria. It was all great, apart from the fact that I used to be quite shy when it came to talking to strangers in bars. Every night I went to a local club called the Whiskeymill. It was a cozy place, a flirting heaven, lots of tourists. But there I stood in a corner, all alone, my mouth glued to my mug of wheat beer. I just couldn't talk to anyone, and I still remember how completely out of place I felt. And I remember, too, how good it felt when someone came up and started talking to me. She was an elderly woman, and she talked to me as if she'd known me forever. She found out everything about me, of course, and I found out that her son owned the ski-lodge. I learned a few things about the ski-lodge business, and even though she is no longer with us, he has remained a valuable contact for me. So now, today, whenever I'm at a social get-together, I always make a beeline to anybody who's standing all alone. This sort of contact often*

*generates the best conversations, and sometimes the best social connec-
tions. Plus, I like to think I'm passing on the good feeling she gave to me.
And why do I do this? Because I think those people standing alone must
feel just like I did back then at the Whiskeymill."*

Your life is full of Whiskeymills — childhood stories, everyday situations or more significant events, personal and professional experiences.
Just sit down and call to mind some of those anecdotes that fit easily into
your speech, and they'll make all the difference for your audience!

Don't rely on second-hand information — tell your own stories!

STEP ELEVEN
Mark Twain

Don't you adore those speakers who nonchalantly let drop one great quotation here, another one there?

One of the best live speeches I ever heard was given by Josef Hattig, former CEO of Beck's brewery. He has everything a great speaker needs: charisma, voice projection, dry humor, and a total lack of 'ums' and 'ahs.' He shared a lot of anecdotes; he moved his body smoothly and expressively. But the one thing struck me most was his use of quotations.

He used about 10 quotations during a 45 minute speech. They added credibility to his presentation, an intellectual touch, and an aspect of creativity. I loved it!

Years later I figured out how he did it. Mr. Hattig probably knows 10 quotations by heart, and he randomly uses them as the opportunities present themselves, judging by his audience and the purpose of his speech.

But — wait a minute! Anyone can learn 10 quotations by heart. It's easy. And you, **The Seven Minute Star**, probably already have a repertoire of at least a few that you could use today, should the situation arise.

A Great Starter — A Great Ending

A good quotation can serve perfectly as your opening sentence!

A speech that starts: *"The greatest failure is not to try!"* [9] has begun in an intriguing way. A speech that begins: *"Winston Churchill once said..."* just cannot be boring.

To create an immediate feeling of suspense, I recommend you use the second pattern and first give the name of the person you're quoting: *"Mahatma Gandhi once said..."* — then you pause several seconds, a rather long pause, and you look at everyone in the audience before you continue: *"Change is the essence of life. Be willing to surrender what you are for what you could become."*

A quotation is also a great way to wrap up a speech. Continuing with the theme you set by mentioning the great Indian leader, you might have talked about how change is important, how listening to others is good

---

[9] Debbie Fields, Founder of Debbie Fields Cookies

but not at the expense of following your dream, and how realizing your dream requires you to keep a strong mind. And all this takes you to your concluding statement: *"Let's take Gandhi as our role model; let's stick to our dreams; let's stay focused in our mind, for he said: 'You can chain me, you can torture me, you can even destroy this body, but you will never imprison my mind.'"*

The Credibility Source

Without credibility, there is no trust. You want to be perceived as a trusted speaker! The great thing about quotations is that their originators tend to have huge amounts of credibility. Think of Lincoln, Gandhi, Martin Luther King, Gorbachev, Cicero, John F. Kennedy, Socrates. Shakespeare quotations like *"Better a witty fool than a foolish wit"* have special power, because they're so well known. You can find one to fit almost any occasion, and using one lends you an intellectual cachet. So borrow some credibility without even being a thief — just make sure you get your quotation right!

Speaking Their Language

Despite the fact that English is the global business language, we all are challenged sometimes by local language barriers. Consider what Nelson Mandela once said: *"If you talk to a man in a language he understands, that goes to his head. If you talk to him in his language, that goes to his heart."* Nelson Mandela is a great man. Audiences are positioned to believe this, so take advantage of it. Strengthen your own point by borrowing the credibility of others.

And Mandela's point about language is right, too. Imagine yourself preparing to do business in Barcelona. If you attend my preparation course, I would tell you that, while Spanish is among the most widely-spoken languages in the world, and is one of the official languages of the United Nations, business people in Barcelona usually prefer to speak, and be addressed, in Catalan. I have never really understood why our Catalonian friends insist so much on their Catalan identity, but they are not the only people in the world who believe that their soul resides in their language. So my advice is that if you want to do business long-term in Barcelona, learn Catalan — at least some of the basics! *Visca Barça!*

Or imagine yourself preparing to do business in Latin America. The Spanish you should use sounds a bit different from the Spanish of Spain. It's good to be aware of this. Or imagine yourself preparing to do business in China. They certainly don't expect you to learn Chinese — at least not right away. But if you can learn to give a Chinese greeting, you'll go a long way toward impressing your audience.

The language you speak has power. You can create a strong bond between yourself and your audience if you make an effort to speak their language, even if it is not your own. Several things happen: they'll appreciate your effort, respect you for your courage and your show of respect for them and their language, and they'll tend to listen to you more carefully and be less critical. They'll also be more forgiving if you make mistakes. Also, an accent is often considered very charming. Think of a Frenchman speaking English — some find it amusing, others find it refreshing, many find it exotic and intriguing. You might win the audience over simply by choosing to speak their language[10].

The Intellect Source

You are *The Seven Minute Star*! You already speak in public, or you soon will. You already are an intellectual, by definition. And yet, it is always good to add something more to what you already have. As my mentor always quotes Voltaire, *"Better is the enemy of good!"*

Famous quotations in any language have become famous because they stand out from the great mass of world literature. Sometimes they're philosophical, sometimes full of puns and fun. A good source of quotations is an intellectual gold mine, full of sparkling nuggets just waiting for you. Mark Twain, for instance, who wrote Huckleberry Finn, is always a superb source of brilliant quotations. On self-esteem he wrote:

---

[10] Note: Speaking the audience's language has two meanings here: 1) The same natural language and 2) use a vocabulary and language they are familiar with and can relate to.

"It shames the average man to be valued below his own estimate of his worth." Or about speaking off the cuff: *"It takes three weeks to write a good impromptu speech."*

It's only common sense. The intellectual quality and value of your speech content will rise if you make good use of quotations.

Quotations are great! Start by learning 10 of them by heart. Then keep adding new ones!

STEP TWELVE
Bob Hope Knew It

The gentleman at your last party — that gentleman who told one joke after another — that gentleman who laughed louder than anyone, but who made everyone around him laugh. That gentleman was funny. You are not!

That is what YOU think. But what if you could make them laugh the same way?

Adding humor to your speech is one of the most delicate steps to becoming **The Seven Minute Star**. Not everyone is a natural entertainer like Ben Stiller. If you are, good, go ahead and skip this step. If you feel like you could improve, let's see what your options are.

Humor Is For Any Occasion

The good news is: you don't have an option![11] You will have to make your audience laugh — because they want to laugh. Everyone wants to laugh. It might be a professional business speech, a speech in court, a wedding speech, even a speech on a sad occasion. Laughter from the audience makes your speech memorable. Humor can help you leave the impression you want.

Where I grew up, a small village in Northern Bavaria, people still talk about the speech I gave at my father's funeral. You might oppose the use of humor during a funeral speech, but you should have known my father: carnival president for 13 years, socializer, joke teller, everybody's favorite. There was no way I was going to deliver yet another tearjerker of a monologue. So I dedicated my introduction to the way my father used to write daily letters to the editors of the local papers: *"The twelfth of March is a tragic day for all of us!"* Confirming nods throughout the church. I continued: *"But today is also a tragic day. We've just been informed that both New Press and Coburg News have filed for Chapter 11 — they ran out of letters to the editor!"*

Of course people are sad at funerals, but I used humor to describe in an authentic way the person they'd known, not the person they'd normally expect to hear about on such an occasion. The congregation ap-

---

[11] Others might have different opinions here.

preciated it, and, remarkably, still remember my speech today. Dare to use humor — on any occasion!

Fall Of The Alpha Dog

At least one top-ranking big shot will be sitting in the front row of any audience. The biggest, the tallest, the richest, the most powerful, the most successful, the biggest star — whatever he is that makes him the "alpha-dog" in that room — he is, straight away, your target.

Let's assume we are not at a TED talk event or at the annual White House Correspondents' Association Dinner. Then it's quite likely your audience hosts a high percentage of underdogs, the more passive sort of characters who look up to the big shot in the first row. Many of them will be envious. The moment you make fun of, or, better, have fun with, the alpha-dog, the audience will laugh with it. But be careful: you're walking on thin ice. The audience has to know that it's all in good fun.

Imagine saying to the President of the US, who's sitting in the first row: *"I was told that the President and I have the same hobby. We both love to run. I love to run away from problems..."*

Comedian Bob Hope would make fun of his assistant at a certain point in his stand-up show, but one time his assistant made a mistake, and made fun of Bob Hope instead. The audience reacted much more enthusiastically than they did to the normal routine, so Bob Hope changed the script.

Imagine the CEO of the Japanese multinational you work for is at your presentation. Well — maybe that isn't such a good idea — but in all other cases, make fun of — with — the big shot in the audience. It'll give everybody a good laugh.

Interact With The Audience

The alpha-dog couldn't escape from your comments. This is a very specific form of one-sided interaction. In general, audiences appreciate it when you involve and interact with them. Most of the time, laughter is the result. During the closing of my Toastmasters contest speech about the attack of little Alvaro (you'll read about him in a moment), I pointed to the dark circles around my eyes and said: *"And even if I have to wear shades on a foggy day..."* — and a lady in the third row started to roar with laughter, because she thought the image I'd built was just so hilarious. I looked at her and made that 'I'm watching you!' gesture like Robert de Niro's in 'Meet The Parents,' and the lady almost fell off her chair.

One technique is to engage in some small-talk with some people from the audience prior to your speech. You can remember a few names and some background information, and then use it during your presentation. Suppose you're talking about the pros and cons of smoking: *"We have people here in this group, like Elisabeth from Arkansas, who are pro smoking. I didn't know that smoking was even allowed in Arkansas. We're also delighted by the presence of opponents like José from Madrid — which is also funny, because I thought all Spaniards were heavy smokers!"* And of course it's all true, in its way. Personalizing the two opposing groups, and adding a humorous touch, helps you win the audience over, not to one side or the other, but to your side.

Make Fun Of Yourself

Once I attended an all-American wedding in Los Angeles. As at other weddings, I wanted to perform my personalized version of "My Way," so I took the mike and started with my intro: *"Germans know how to build cars. Germans know how to make beer. Germans know how to drink beer. But there is one thing Germans do not know how to do. Germans don't know how to be funny. I am not funny, and I will not try and pathetically entertain you..."* It made 160 wedding guests laugh.

During my time at KPMG I used to point out: *"Of our 120,000 employees in 148 countries, I am the only one who has never calculated a Cash Flow!"* The best weakness is the one you address publicly. Keep your ace hidden up your sleeve until you need it, though. But play it at the right time —make fun of yourself— and the audience will love it!

Tell A Joke

Maybe you couldn't tell a joke even if your life depended on it. But each of us has at least one or two favorite jokes. Why not tell one of them, maybe even as your opening sentence? But make sure your joke is not going to be offensive, and that it fits well with your presentation. You don't want to lose three quarters of your audience in the first 30 seconds. Search the web for topic-related jokes. You'll find plenty of them for any topic. But sometimes the best place to look first for a good joke is in your own life.

Making Funny Faces

You remember the mirror from Step 7? You were searching for your smile. But you can use facial expressions for a lot more than smiling. When you talk about dull people passing by in a street bar, make a dull face. When you talk about the biggest frown you ever saw on your boss's face, share it with the audience. Make sure you make these faces for at least three looooong seconds. It will take a little while before everyone in the room will understand your little drama. The moment you begin to think you've overdone it, it's time to stop! Perfect! I recommend that you experiment with your funny faces for a while. You're the best judge of the reactions you'll get.

Exaggerate

- *"Even my paycheck is bigger than the help provided to the victims of Katrina."*
- *"I ran 734,999 miles to attend this meeting, and I am still late!"*
- *"On September 13th 2006, Alvaro Mueck Conde attacked me, attacked my wife, and attacked our families in a severe, sudden and unexpected strike! Sure, there had been rumors for, oh, nine months or so, that something was about to happen. But we refused to believe them; we wanted to keep the peace. The aftermath of Alvaro's attack can only be described as: absolute*

devastation. Friends — gone. Romantic dinners — history.
Nightlife — destroyed!"

Exaggerations are humorous aspects of a speech that are easy-to-build.
You can find examples almost anywhere. *"Aren't you tired of those guys*
who show off with their 76-hour work day and 536-hour work-week? You
better pray they aren't lawyers!"

Exaggerate! Make everything incredibly, outrageously, abominably
bigger: the numbers, the sizes, the weights, the distances, the speeds, the
dangers, the fears....

Humor is an essential element of any speech. And in case you didn't
know it: you ARE funny!

STEP THIRTEEN
2 Michaels, 1 Ali

In your opinion, what characteristics do great speakers share?

When I ask my seminar participants this question, they mostly come up with a list of about ten characteristics.

These are mentioned regularly:
- Charisma
- Credibility
- Authenticity

They also value:
- Transparency
- Drive
- Ability to move and to engage the crowd
- Consistency in the message

Despite small differences from seminar to seminar, one characteristic consistently shows up on the list: great speakers have ***enthusiasm.***

I asked an American friend once what the difference is between en-thusiasm and passion. He explained that somebody who's enthusiastic really wants to make something happen. It's a joyful, goal-driven at-titude. Passion on the other hand is an intrinsic love for something. I'll talk about passion in the next step.

Just like your smile, enthusiasm is contagious. But you'll only per-suade, motivate or inspire your audience when they feel that you are en-thusiastic about your topic.

How do you make them feel your enthusiasm?

The Glass Is Half-Full
Every day newspapers overflow with negative headlines. But leave the negative vibes to the media. You are *The Seven Minute Star*. Your audi-ence wants to hear an uplifting and engaging speech filled with positivity. An enthusiast is, by definition, a positive person for whom the glass will

always be half-full.

Yet about half of us perceive a half-full glass as being half-empty instead. What about these people? And what about — you? Is your glass half-full, or half-empty?

The owner of the kindergarten that my son used to attend once told us: *"The personality of your children is formed between the day they are born and the time they turn three. That's it!"* Since that lady had 25 years of experience, nobody would doubt her words. What this means is that if you perceive your glass as half-empty, it will always be half-empty. If you say *"But..."* a lot, you'll always say it. However, there's hope. We all have a magnificent brain; we all have something called reason. You can tell your brain, even if only for the next seven minutes, that yours will be a glass that's half-full!

Whatever your personality, on stage you will be positive — always!

Body & Voice

You remember your voice, the sensitive beast? Now the moment has come to let it out of its cage.

And your body? Now it is time to overdo it!

Your two main ingredients to help you serve a delicious plate of enthusiasm are your voice and your body movements.

Just think about the singing, preaching, demanding, intriguing, and goose-bump-inducing "I Have A Dream" speech by Dr. Martin Luther King, Jr. When he cried out, *"Let freedom ring,"* both his voice and his body were overwhelming in their enthusiasm. Half a million people at the Lincoln Memorial could feel it. The world could feel it.

When you talk about the injustice of racial segregation, your voice must be resonant, fuelled by your own disappointment, disgust and anger. Your message must reflect your absolute determination!

When you speak in front of the Board about the goals you want to accomplish with your business unit, raise your voice every time you say, *"We will...!"*

When you speak about how to gain more self-confidence, think of Tony Robbins, and emulate his firm, determined voice.

You can buttress nearly any message with body language:

When you talk about the goal you'll score in the next fiscal year, precede your statement with a kick.

Before you say that you'll go right to the top with your company, point your finger and look up at the ceiling.

Clap your hands loudly once, then say: *"It will be a clash of cultures!"*

Your vocal variety and your body language make your enthusiasm visible, audible and tangible. They bring your enthusiasm to life. Set them free!

Learn From The Best

How would Formula One car racing legend Michael Schumacher talk about that one millisecond better time?

How would Michael Jordan talk about that one impossible three-point basket in the final second?

How would Mohammed Ali talk about that one final, decisive punch?

Next time you present a market analysis, imagine presenting it the way Michael Schumacher would explain the latest evolution in Formula One racecar design. How would your analysis sound then? Enthusiasm takes over. You'll be thrilled to tell your colleagues about all the great opportunities that new market conditions are opening up for you. And you might add: *"Let's unleash the final punch straight to the jaw of our competitors!"*

Imagine telling your best friend about your newborn daughter — then share that same enthusiasm with your audience!

STEP FOURTEEN
It's All About Love

Why did people hang on Mother Theresa's every word when she lectured about caring for those in need?

Why is Steven Spielberg the most sought after keynote speaker?

How can Benjamin Zander convince thousands of people to start liking classical music?

How could John F. Kennedy move an entire country with a single rhetorical flourish?

In one sentence: They love what they do, and they love to speak about it.

Your audience can be a fierce critic. They can sense a fake attitude. If you talk about something without showing passion, they'll say, *"That dog don't hunt!"*.

There is only one way to make them feel your passion. You have to talk about something you really love!

Add Passion To Your Speech

You create your own speech — at least you should. You control your content, so only you can add passion to it.

A friend once told me that the next day she was going to present the monthly marketing update to the head of her business unit. She managed a shampoo brand. As we talked about it, I learned that she always enjoys bubble-baths, and she particularly enjoys using her product. So I recommended that she start her presentation unlike the usual way. Weeks later I met her again; with a big smile, she reflected on how she'd opened her presentation: *"I understand our customers. I know why they love our product. Yesterday I took a bubble-bath. I don't know when is the last time you took one using our shampoo, but it feels just wonderful! It's so smooth, so relaxing, and this scent of 1,000 tropical islands.... I love our product! That's why I'm not surprised that last month's results once again beat the forecast."*

My friend turned a dull, number-based presentation into an emotional experience — with passion! And her boss loved it.

You can add bits and pieces of passion to any speech content. Remember how I compared KPMG's organizational structure to a soccer team (Step 9). I love soccer, so whenever I use it as a metaphor, I can sound passionate about what I'm saying.

What about your passion? Is it skiing, opera, golf, ballet, travel, your job, your family, your friends?

Imagine you are to talk about the importance of client relationships in service marketing. Why not compare your clients with your friends? *"The number one value for me in a friendship is mutual trust. Consider my friend Dennis. Dennis is credible — I believe what he says. I also value his reliability. When I was having marital problems, Dennis invited me to Paris! Dennis is always there for me. I also appreciate our intimacy. I know what you're thinking of now, but no, I mean our shared experiences. We've shared a lot of adventures together. When I say something, Dennis knows what I mean. Finally, friendship is about giving, not about taking. I've never had the feeling that Dennis was using me for his own benefit. We're just very good friends. I trust Dennis!"*

You can copy this trust analogy and paste it into any client relationship in the service industry[12]. Where there is mutual trust between service provider and customer, there is business. But it needn't be said that you'll sound much more passionate when you're talking about your friend.

Are you an opera fan? Create a passionate speech in three acts using the corresponding metaphors.

Do you love to play golf? Compare the tension you feel when you organize an annual general meeting with standing on the green: *"You prepare everything. You consider all possible factors — the wind, the decline, the ground friction, the humidity, the ball, the putt speed. And still, you can never be 100% sure that the ball will make it into that damn hole!"*

You can add passion to any speech!

---

[12] See Maister, Galford, and Green, The Trusted Advisor (2002)

And If You Don't Love It?

Difficult question. If at all possible, I recommend that you only speak about topics you can identify with 100%. I remember once I had to organize a presentation for my former boss dealing with the evolution of the global insurance market from the perspective of Mergers & Acquisitions. I love my mentor, but the insurance market was clearly not one of his top priorities. The speech was a calamity. The self-explanatory slides could have balanced out the way he didn't understand what he was talking about, but he just simply looked bored and annoyed. It was painfully obvious, and it was not a good attitude to have in front of 500 MBA students.

Top executives have to give speeches and presentations all the time. The best thing to do is to add personal anecdotes from your own areas of interest and passion to spice up any given content, for yourself as well as for your audience.

Write Your Own Content

The insurance speech given by my former boss was, of course, prepared by someone else. Fabian was a young go-getter and a true professional. He loved the presentation he put together, and would have given it with passion.

Time is our most precious commodity, so you might believe that you should have other people prepare your speeches. I could not disagree more. When you speak in public, you expose yourself completely, as well as the company you represent. Isn't crafting the perception you'll create more important than spending a few more hours planning the budget?

You should always find the time to prepare your own speeches — on the plane, in the taxi, in your hotel room somewhere in Charlotte, North Carolina. The simple fact is, you will always exude more passion when you show your own emotions, use your own words, and be yourself.

Speak from the heart when it matters most.

STEP FIFTEEN
Eid, Hanukkah, Christmas

You might wonder why something as banal as your smile makes it the 15th and probably the most significant step to becoming *The Seven Minute Star*. I was saving the best for last! Don't underestimate your smile. It's your magical gift to your audience. Your smile is contagious. Your smile expresses trust, warmth, and positivity.

When do you normally smile? You smile when you see a friend in the street. You smile when you embrace your three year-old daughter. You smile when you see something comical on TV. You smile when you read a funny headline in the newspaper in the coffee shop next door. You could smile in a coffee shop in Amsterdam for other reasons, and you might even smile when you see your mother-in-law.

But when you step on stage, you don't smile! Why not?

www.TED.com is probably the best online source today for experiencing the most charismatic speakers in the world. Have you ever seen Tony Robbins not smiling? Have you seen Rory Sutherland not smiling? Have you seen Benjamin Zander not smiling? No — they all are smiling at you because they're aware of the invisible power of their smile.

When is the last time you saw yourself smiling? Exactly. You know, you'd better get your smile back. Your days of stepping up to the lectern sporting a horizontal line of indifference across your face are over.

The First Moment Of Truth

In Step 3 you learned that you should take your time and wait until the audience is covered by a sheet of absolute silence before you actually start speaking. These are the 3 to 5 seconds which build up to the first moment of truth. These are the 3 to 5 seconds during which you deliver your first impression to your audience. Imagine that — it happens even before you begin to speak!

I strongly recommend that you use the time well, to create a likeable image by telegraphing a warm smile to your audience. As Rory Sutherland says, it's all about perception!

The Last Moment Of Truth

People remember best the very first moments of your speech, and the last. So the last moment of truth approaches as you whisper the last syllables to a, by then, informed, persuaded, motivated or inspired audience. Again, you will pass your special gift on to them — your smile. The final message of any speech must be uplifting. Your smile works with almost any ending[13].

Positive Message – Positive Face

Although people tend not to pay too much attention to what they perceive positively, still, you can be sure they will react negatively to an indifferent or sad expression when you talk about the great achievements your company has made during the last decade.

Accompany your positive messages with a smile. It always makes the impact even stronger.

You're Always Selling Yourself

Finally, what changes a good sales person into a great sales person?

Forget about product knowledge, engineering skill, diplomas, degrees, and certificates. A great sales person is a likeable person, an empathetic person, someone you'd like to have join you for a beer in the bar around the corner. You can talk about almost anything — the last Superbowl, your recent divorce, your children. Have you ever seen a person like that who wasn't wearing a big fat friendly smile?

When you speak in public, you might be selling an idea, you might be selling your company, or you might be selling your department, but always, invariably, inevitably, you're selling yourself! You too are one of those great salespeople. Learn from them! Smile!

You give away presents on Eid, Hanukkah, or Christmas. Give your smile away to your audience all the time! The more you give it away, the more of it you have to give.

---

[13] There are certain speeches for which it is not appropriate to end with a smile, such as when you declare war or announce that catastrophe has struck. Body language must always be authentic, must agree with the message, and must conform to your objective.

GREAT,
BUT WHAT ABOUT AUTHENTICITY?

You've come a long way. All 15 challenging steps lie behind you:

You smile now the way you did when you were a kid. You are passionate about the content you share with your audience. Enthusiasm flows through your veins. You make people laugh. You surprise the audience with your quotations and anecdotes. You have sharpened your rhetorical weapons. You skip all the boring stuff and get to the point. You spice up your speech with everyday objects. You support your message with meaningful body language. Your voice has turned into a sensitive beast. You look deeply into all those eyes peering up from down below. You take those Rottweilers by the leash with your first sentence. You touch people's emotions by opening yourself up more than you ever have before, and you impress the audience with your abundance of self-confidence!

Doesn't it seem strange to you that, when it comes to public speaking, one of the major concerns people have can't be found in any of these 15 steps?

No, they are afraid of something completely different. They are afraid of not being authentic. Authenticity seems to be the biggest challenge for many public speakers moving up the staircase of their speaking career.

According to the Merriam-Webster definition, 'authentic' means, among other things: worthy of acceptance or belief; not false or imitation; true to one's own personality, spirit or character.

At this stage of the book, you have walked up all those 15 steps. You will have realized that, once you have climbed them all, automatically you are authentic. Steps 2, 9, 10, 12, 13, 14, and 15 all demand that you be true to your own personality, spirit, and character.

You are authentic by being transparent, by sharing some of your sacred moments and emotions with the audience, by telling your anecdotes, by interacting with the audience, by showing enthusiasm for what you intend to accomplish, by being passionate, and most important, by giving away your most sincere smile.

Dear Master Speaker: I would like to congratulate you! Not only are you *The Seven Minute Star* — now you are *The Authentic Seven Minute Star!*

I cannot wait to see you on stage. And by the way, if you want to join me at Cats Meow in New Orleans, just drop me a line!

APPENDIX THE SPEECH DEVELOPMENT TEMPLATE
CREATE YOUR SPEECH IN JUST 5 MINUTES!

I: Create titles for the most interesting facets of your topic and write them in the rectangles.

II: Choose the three most striking facets of your topic and mark crosses in the corresponding triangles.

III: Think about the logical order (e.g. oldest to newest) for the three chosen facets and add an A, a B and a C in the corresponding circle.

IV: Enter the ABC titles in the three columns of the speech structure building below. Add bullet points, the first sentence/intro and the closing. Ready!

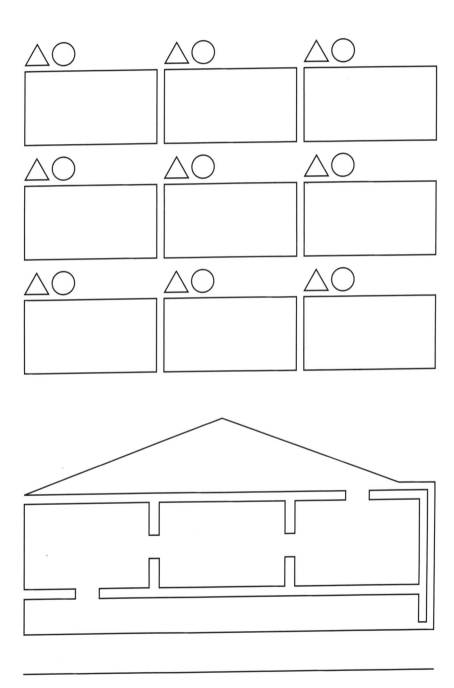

THE STEP INDEX

THE STAR INDEX

ABOUT THE WRITER

Florian Mueck is co-founder and director of thefestival.eu – an initiative to bring the European idea to life. Before coming up with the idea to create this movement, this entrepreneur, based in Barcelona, Spain, and Berlin, Germany, was working for 8 years as a consultant and business development manager for KPMG, the global advisory firm.

Public speaking has always been Florian's most important tool for making things happen in all his activities. Since he joined a chapter of Toastmasters International in Barcelona in 2005, public speaking, already his passion, has become his profession.

Florian's speaking style is fueled by humor and acting, and he is well known for his extemporaneous speaking as well. He offers entertaining one-day public-speaking seminars and keynote speeches based on the 15 steps to becoming *The Seven Minute Star*.

More information on Florian Mueck you will find on www.linkedin.com, www.xing.com, www.thefestival.eu, and www.thesevenminutestar.com.

Made in the USA
Lexington, KY
24 May 2014